Third Edition

TRUE GRIST

Patricia B. Mitchell

D1824562

Buckwheat Flour
and
Cornmeal Recipes

Published 1992 by the author at the Sims-Mitchell
House Bed & Breakfast, 242 Whittle Street SW, P. O.
Box 429, Chatham, VA 24531 (804-432-0595).

Printed in the U. S. A.
ISBN 0-925117-53-6

Second Printing, August 1992

- Note from the Author -

To **millers** and **molinologists**: As a food historian
and author who especially esteems grist mills and bread,
I am constantly looking for information about historic
mills and for old-fashioned recipes utilizing whole grains.
If you would be willing to share such material with me, I
would be deeply appreciative.

- Patricia B. Mitchell

TABLE OF CONTENTS

* * * * * * * * * * * * * * * *

INTRODUCTION

This land was once generously dotted with grist mills, most of which have now vanished or lie in crumbled ruins. At the few which are still in operation, however, we can not only observe millers engaged in their business, but we can also purchase the fruit of their labors. Stone-ground (or buhr-ground or water-ground -- the terms are interchangeable) meal has more intense, robust flavor, and stone-ground meal is more nutritious than most store-bought meal which is over-processed and less than fresh.

In this cookbook we will concentrate on two grist mill products, buckwheat flour and cornmeal. Buckwheat was brought to this country by the Dutch in the early 1600's. Cornmeal is an indigenous crop, corn or maize having been a staple of the Native Americans.

After touring a grist mill and buying a sack of just-ground meal, do not merely take the bag home and set it on a shelf as a souvenir. Open it! Use it! Buckwheat flour is renowned as a flavorful and appealing component of hot cakes. It can also be used in combination with various grains in baked goods, and can be served as a breakfast cereal. Cornmeal is useful in everything from Indian pudding to corn dogs, from turkey stuffing to tamale pie; and in a myriad of baked goods. Who doesn't enjoy classic corn bread, corn pones, and corn muffins, "with the ever-alluring fresh-from-the-oven-taste!" (as an advertisement for Kellogg's Toasted Corn Flakes described their product in the May 22, 1915 *Saturday Evening Post*). Indeed, home-cooked foods, made from newly-ground meal do have an "ever-alluring fresh-from-the-oven-taste," so start cookin' and enjoy!

* * * * * * * * * * * * * * * *

RAISED BUCKWHEAT GRIDDLE CAKES

Call 'em griddle cakes, batter cakes, flapjacks, pancakes, crepes, blintzes, or chapaties, these flat, thin circles of fried batter are deservedly popular, and have been so for centuries. -- Remember to flip them only once. They are delicious served with honey or maple syrup, butter, applesauce, or even dollops of yogurt!

* * *

3 c. buckwheat flour
1 c. all-purpose, unbleached, or whole wheat flour
1 tsp. salt
1 pkg. baking yeast
1 tsp. sugar or honey
2 tbsp. brown sugar or molasses
3/4 tsp. baking soda
1 tbsp. vegetable oil

Combine flours and salt in a large bowl. Soften yeast in 1/4 c. warm water. Combine sugar or honey with 3 3/4 c. warm water; mix with yeast mixture. Stir into dry ingredients. Cover; let stand overnight at room temperature. [Note: the bowl should be only half full at first, because the batter will expand.]

The next a.m. stir in brown sugar or molasses, soda, and oil. Reserve 1 c. batter for starter for the next batch.* Cook remaining batter on a hot, lightly-greased griddle. Makes 20 pancakes.

*To use starter, remove cup of reserved batter from refrigerator (where it keeps well for several weeks), and add 1 c. lukewarm water, 1/2 c. buckwheat flour, and 1/2 c. all-purpose, unbleached, or whole wheat flour. Stir well. Let stand overnight. When ready to use, add 1/2 tsp. salt, 1/2 tsp. soda, 2 tbsp. brown sugar or molasses, and 1 tbsp. vegetable oil. Again, reserve 1 c. of the batter for the next batch.

QUICK BUCKWHEAT FLAPJACKS

The recipe on the preceding page requires advance planning because of the yeast. Quick Buckwheat Flapjacks are a spur-of-the-moment winner. Incidentally, there is no law that flapjacks must be served only at breakfast. Try them for a light lunch or easy supper. Any extras can be frozen, and reheated by popping in a toaster for a few seconds; or, if you plan to use them soon, don't freeze, just reheat in the oven when needed.

* * *

3/4 c. buckwheat flour
1/2 c. wheat germ
1/4 c. whole wheat flour
1 3/4 tsp. baking powder
2 eggs, beaten
3 tbsp. vegetable oil
3 tbsp. molasses
Milk

Combine dry ingredients. In a separate bowl mix liquids, adding enough milk to make the batter the consistency of heavy cream. Cook on a hot griddle. Yield: 10 pancakes.

BUCKWHEAT HISTORY

Buckwheat, incidentally, originally grew in Asia, and has been cultivated in China for centuries. From Asia buckwheat was taken to Europe, and from Europe to the New World. In the 1860's buckwheat was an important U. S. crop with an annual yield of 23 million bushels. Now much less is grown. The chief growing region is in the eastern states.

Buckwheat can be cultivated on land that is too wet for other grains. Sometimes farmers plant it late in the spring in cornfields that have been destroyed by frost or by other causes.

BUCKWHEAT CREPES

These thin pancakes can be filled with cream cheese, ricotta or cottage cheese, fruit, jam, syrup, herring in sour cream (!), cooked meats, whatever you crave.

* * *

3 eggs, well-beaten
1 c. sour milk or buttermilk (or enough to make a thin batter)
1/2 c. buckwheat flour
1/4 c. whole wheat flour
1 tbsp. butter or margarine, melted

When the eggs have been thoroughly beaten, beat in the remaining ingredients. Beat out lumps. Let batter sit at least an hour before using. For each crêpe, pour about 1/4 c. batter into a greased skillet, swirling the batter over the bottom of the pan to form a thin pancake. Cook over medium-high heat, flipping only once. Fold each cooked crêpe into quarters. -- After filling, roll up (like a scroll).

GOOF-PROOF BUCKWHEAT CAKES

I expected that a recipe calling for 100% buckwheat flour would produce a somewhat substantial (read "heavy") pancake with a very pronounced (read "strong") buckwheat flavor. Boy, was I wrong! These fluffy buck-jacks are pleasantly mild-tasting and delicious. I serve them as a supper dish topped with creamed chicken (or turkey). We like relatively thick pancakes when used as a base for an entree, so I make them about 1/3-inch thick. If you prefer a "crêpe-ier" pancake, thin the uncooked batter with additional milk.

* * *

2 c. buckwheat flour
1 tbsp. baking powder
2 tsp. sugar
3/4 tsp. salt

1 egg, beaten
2 c. milk
2 tbsp. vegetable oil (or melted butter or margarine)

Combine the dry ingredients. In a separate bowl, beat together the wet ingredients. Combine the two mixtures, mixing well. Pour approximately 1/4 c. of batter for each pancake out onto a hot greased griddle or skillet. When bubbles appear on the surface, flip. (Not yourself, the griddle cakes!) Stack on a plate covered with aluminum foil to keep warm until time to serve. (As I said, we love these with creamed chicken on top.)

BUCKWHEAT BREAKFAST CEREAL

I first came across this recipe in a cookbook for campers. The stick-to-the-ribs character of this dish does make it an excellent choice for those "hitting the trail," or engaging in other vigorous physical exercise. If you really feel rugged, eat this breakfast cereal as recommended for campers -- with scallions and soy sauce! (Old timers in the mountains liked raw chopped onions with their breakfast grits. Obviously they had strong constitutions!)

* * *

1 1/2 c. buckwheat flour
3 c. boiling water
1/4 - 1/2 tsp. salt

Toast buckwheat flour in a large skillet for about five minutes. Remove from burner and pour on boiling water. Add salt, and mix well. Eat as-is, or add milk.

BUCKWHEAT LATKES

Latkes are a traditional Jewish food, especially associated with Chanukah. These battercakes are often made with grated potatoes, but buckwheat is a fine choice, too! Serve with applesauce.

* * *

1 pkg. baking yeast
2 c. warm water
1 tbsp. sugar or honey
2 c. warm milk
1 tsp. salt (or less to suit your taste)
3 1/4 c. buckwheat flour

1/2 c. all-purpose, unbleached, or whole wheat flour
1/4 c. vegetable oil
2 tbsp. honey
1/4 tsp. baking soda
1 egg, beaten

Combine the first six ingredients. Beat, cover, and let rise overnight. In the morning, add the remaining five ingredients. Beat. Cook on a greased griddle or in a skillet.

A-DROP-IN-THE-BUCKWHEAT BISCUITS

If you've read many of my cookbooks, you know I'm wild about drop biscuits! Here's my version of he-man, mouth-watering buckwheat biscuits.

* * *

2 c. whole wheat flour
1 c. wheat germ
1 c. buckwheat flour
1 scant tsp. salt
1 1/2 tbsp. baking powder
1/3 c. vegetable oil
Approximately 2 c. milk, more or less

Mix dry ingredients. Add milk to oil to equal two cups. Pour liquid into dry ingredients, adding more milk if necessary. Drop large spoonfuls onto greased baking sheets. Bake at 425° F. for 10-12 minutes, being cautious not to over-brown the bottoms.

LITTLE RASCAL BUCKWHEAT MUFFINS

Buckwheat is a highly nutritious cereal grass containing lots of B vitamins, potassium, phosphorus, sulphur, and carbohydrates. It is the only food source of rutin (which is similar to bioflavonoids). Rutin is often combined with vitamin C as a dietary supplement tablet. It helps to protect vitamin C in the body, and may also aid in strengthening capillary walls, and building resistance to infections and colds.

These light, airy muffins almost seem to whisper, "Please pass the butter!"

* * *

1/2 c. buckwheat flour
1/4 c. soy flour
1/4 c. brown rice flour
1 1/2 tsp. baking powder
1/2 tsp. salt
1 tbsp. vegetable oil
1 tbsp. molasses
1 egg, beaten
1 c. buttermilk or sour milk

Mix dry ingredients. In a separate bowl, mix liquid ingredients. Combine the two mixtures, beating out lumps. Pour into greased muffin tins and bake at 425° F. for approximately 12 minutes. Yield: 1 dozen muffins.

THE BEST BRAWNY BANANA BUCKWHEAT BREAD

This tempting bread has a tender texture and a tantalizing, almost mysterious flavor. The unusual combination of bananas, buckwheat, and soy creates a subtle yet intense taste that is sure to please. Serve warm for breakfast.

My children Sarah and David, when sampling this recipe for the first time, both announced, "Buy some more buckwheat flour, Mom!" -- They obviously were enthusiastic about The Best Brawny Banana Buckwheat Bread!

* * *

1/4 c. warm water
1 tbsp. baking yeast
1/4 c. honey

2 eggs, beaten
1/4 c. vegetable oil
1/2 tsp. vanilla
3 very ripe bananas, mashed
1 1/2 c. buckwheat flour
1/2 c. soy flour
1/4 tsp. salt
1/4 c. pecans, chopped

Mix the first three ingredients, and let set five minutes. Meanwhile, combine the remaining ingredients in a large bowl. Add the yeast mixture. Beat together thoroughly, and spoon into a greased and floured loaf pan. Let sit for half an hour, then bake at 350° F. for about one hour. To test for doneness, insert a toothpick near the center of the loaf. If the bread is baked, no sticky batter will remain on the toothpick when it's pulled out of the loaf. Yield: 1 loaf.

GLORIFIED BUCKWHEAT LOAVES

The buckwheat plant grows about three feet tall and has heart-shaped leaves. The clustered flowers are small and fragrant -- either white, or white tinged with pink, or pale red. Each flower produces a single triangular gray or black seed.

Buckwheat has few pests or diseases, and requires no fertilizer (which would stimulate excess leaf growth and reduction of seed yield). Insecticides are avoided in order to protect the pollinating bees. It requires little cultivation and thrives on poor soil. Let's encourage its production by consuming more of this tasty *POLYGONACEAE FAGOPYRUM*! -- Incidentally, every autumn there is a buckwheat festival in Preston County, West Virginia.

* * *

1/2 c. warm water
1 tbsp. baking yeast
2 c. warm water
1/4 c. dry milk powder
3/4 c. raisins and 1/2 c. sunflower seeds, chopped finely
5 c. or more whole wheat flour
1 c. buckwheat
1 1/2 tsp. salt

Mix the yeast in the 1/2 c. warm water. When it froths up, add other ingredients. Form a ball and knead on a floured surface until smooth. In a cozy spot, allow to rise in a greased bowl until doubled in size. Punch down, and form two loaves. Place in greased loaf pans. Cover. Let rise again. Just before baking, brush 2 tbsp. water over each loaf. Bake at 350° F. for approximately one hour. Serve warm with butter or margarine or try buckwheat honey -- a very dark, distinctive honey, said to be the most nutritious of all honeys! Yield: 2 loaves.

REALLY RARE BUCKWHEAT RYE BREAD

As you may have discovered, recipes utilizing buckwheat flour are rather rare; and to find one recipe incorporating both buckwheat and rye flours is really astonishing! In this bold-flavored bread, the two flours complement each other, with the essence of buckwheat standing out as the more pronounced sensation.

By the way, you will notice that whole wheat flour is also utilized in this recipe, whole wheat flour being a much wiser choice (from the nutritional point of view) than white flour. Since the days of early Rome, the affluent have opted for white flour rather than the brown flour of whole grains in order to show their prestige. (In the distant past, refined flours cost more than the "less tampered-with" dark flour, which still contains its bran and wheat germ.)

In 13th-century Arabian courts, a lavish repast of roast kid, wine, and white bread was the mark of utmost self-indulgence -- however, as you've noticed, I certainly advocate the use of whole grain flours whenever possible because of their superior nutrition and taste. (In the past decade we "baby boomers" have influenced the market because the demand for whole grain bread is up dramatically, while the demand for white bread has dropped.)

* * *

1 pkg. baking yeast
2 c. warm water
1/4 c. molasses
1/4 c. vegetable oil
1 tsp. salt
2 c. buckwheat flour
2 c. rye flour
2 c. (approximately) whole wheat flour

Combine the first three ingredients. When the mixture froths up, stir in the remaining ingredients, adding more whole wheat flour if necessry to produce a workable dough. Knead vigorously, then place in a greased bowl. Cover and keep slightly warm until the dough doubles in bulk. Punch down and shape into two loaves. Put into greased bread pans. Cover and let rise until light. Bake at 375° F. for approximately 40 minutes, or until the loaves sound hollow when tapped.

"THE BUCKWHEAT STOPS HERE" BREAD

The mellow and unique flavor of buckwheat enhances this yeast loaf bread. "The Buckwheat Stops Here" Bread is a champion for breakfast -- it will provide you with lots of energy. (I also like it with peanut butter, as a snack.) -- Oh, by the way, my husband, when discussing with me the preparation of this bread, quipped Truman-esquely, "Tell 'em if they can't stand the heat, get out of the kitchen!"

* * *

2 pkgs. baking yeast
4 c. warm water
1/2 c. honey
1/3 c. dry milk powder
1/4 c. vegetable oil
1 1/2 tsp. salt
3 c. buckwheat flour
6 1/2 c. (or more) whole wheat flour

In a large mixing bowl, dissolve the yeast in the warm water. Add honey, dry milk powder, oil, salt, and buckwheat flour. Beat well. Gradually add the whole wheat flour, using enough to make moderately stiff dough. Knead on a floured board 5 to 7 minutes. Form a ball and put in a greased bowl, turned to grease all surfaces. Let rise in a warm place 'til double in size. Punch down, form two loaves, and place in greased 9x5-inch loaf pans. Let rise to tops of pans. Bake at 350° F. for 50-60 minutes. Yield: 2 loaves.

SCRAPPLE

My husband and I first encountered this scrumptious breakfast meat on the island of Chincoteague (famous for Pony Penning Day and *Misty of Chincoteague*). Why a seafood restaurant open for fishermen's breakfasts had a Pennsylvania Dutch treat on the menu, I do not know, but I'm glad they did. We ordered it, and have loved it ever since. If you want to make your own, here's how.

* * *

1 1/2 lbs. pork liver
1 1/2 lbs. pork (back bones and feet are good to include, too)
2 1/2 qts. water
4 c. buckwheat flour, sifted

2 c. cornmeal
1/4 tsp. sage
1/2 tsp. salt
1/8 tsp. pepper

In a large pot combine liver and pork; cover with water and boil until tender. Remove meat, and let broth cool. Skim fat off the surface of the broth. Chop or grind the meat and return it to the broth. Add seasonings. Bring to a boil. In a separate bowl combine flour and cornmeal, and slowly pour it into the broth, stirring constantly. Boil for one hour, stirring often. Pour into loaf pans and chill.

To serve, slice, dip in wheat germ, flour, or crumbs, and fry on both sides on a hot greased griddle or in a skillet.

Note: Spices can be varied to suit your taste. Some like more sage, and salt and pepper; or the addition of parsley, rosemary, and/or thyme.

SHORT-CUT SCRAPPLE

If the previous recipe presents too much of a challenge, here is a simple version.

* * *

1 c. cornmeal
3/4 tsp. salt
1 c. cold water
3 c. boiling water
1 lb. bulk sausage, crumbled, cooked, and drained

Combine cornmeal, salt, and cold water; pour into boiling water, stirring vigorously. Return to a boil, stirring constantly. Lower heat, cover, and cook about ten minutes, stirring occasionally. Mix in the sausage meat, creating Short-Cut Scrapple.

Rinse a loaf pan with cold water, and pour in the scrapple mixture. Cool slightly; cover and refrigerate several hours or overnight. To serve, cut into slices and pan-fry in a small amount of butter or margarine until golden brown, about ten minutes per side.

Interesting tidbit: Dwight D. Eisenhower, beloved President during the 1950's, relished crusty Philadelphia scrapple for breakfast.

BUCKWHEAT-CORNMEAL PANCAKES

Back on the subject of buckwheat, buckwheat is related to rhubarb, as well as to dock and other weeds! About cornmeal, the cornmeal which is commercially available nowadays is either yellow, white, or blue. Yellow cornmeal is ground from yellow corn. (It contains vitamin A, which white cornmeal lacks.) White cornmeal is ground from white corn. Blue cornmeal is ground from kernels of corn which are deep blue with a purple tinge. (In colonial days and before, the Indians grew black, white, red, yellow, blue, and multicolored corn. To them, the different colors represented north, south, east, west, zenith, and nadir.) Blue cornmeal tastes somewhat nuttier than yellow or white. (It is also more dense, so use 3/4 cup of blue for every cup of yellow or white in recipes, and increase the flour by 1/4 cup.) The blue corn yields a grayish lavender-colored meal which is 7% lower in fat, and 21% higher in protein than the more commonly used yellow or white cornmeal.

* * *

3/4 c. buckwheat flour
1/4 c. cornmeal
1 tsp. baking powder
1/4 tsp. salt
1 egg, beaten
1 c. buttermilk or sour milk
1 tbsp. vegetable oil

Combine dry ingredients in a bowl. In another bowl, combine liquids. Add slowly to dry ingredients and stir. Drop batter on a hot greased griddle. When bubbles appear on the surface, flip over. Serve with butter and syrup. Yield: 6-8 pancakes.

FORTIFIED CORNMEAL MUSH

Cornmeal mush is "the food which made America great," according to Frank Sieglinger, husband of nutritionist Adelle Davis. He was referring to the fact that cornmeal mush was popular in colonial America -- the founding fathers and their families ate this nourishing breakfast dish [which they called "samp(e)" or "loblolly."]

In 20th-century overseas relief operations, the life-sustaining and body-building value of corn is still appreciated. A porridge of corn and soy is often used to feed third world children in refugee camps. Eat a bowl of this inexpensive, nutritious Fortified Cornmeal Mush and be thankful for a full tummy!

* * *

2/3 c. cornmeal
1/2 c. dry milk powder
1/4 tsp. salt
2/3 c. cold water or milk
2 c. boiling water

Combine the first three ingredients. Stir the 2/3 c. water into the first mixture. Add to, stirring constantly, the 2 c. boiling water. Lower heat. Cover, and cook 5-10 minutes, stirring occasionally. Serve hot with honey or maple syrup, and milk, if desired. Yield: 3 or 4 servings.

Note: To make fried mush, rinse a loaf pan with cold water, and pour the cooked mush made from the above recipe into the loaf pan. Cool, cover, and refrigerate for several hours or overnight. To prepare, cut mush into slices and pan-fry in a small amount of butter or margarine for about 10 minutes per side (until golden brown). Serve hot with honey or syrup.

A NOTE ON EARLY RISING

Speaking of breakfast, I love this quaint quote (and I agree, too)!

"Early rising is also essential to the good government of a family. A late breakfast deranges the whole business of the day, and throws a portion of it on the next, which opens the door for confusion to enter."

- by Mary Randolph
  (19th-century cookbook writer)

CHEESED-UP CORNMEAL MUSH

Akin to the northern Italian favorite, polenta, this belly-warmer serves as a satisfying side dish.

* * *

1 1/2 c. yellow cornmeal
4 1/2 c. water
1 tsp. salt
1/2 stick butter or margarine
1/2 c. Parmesan cheese

Put one cup of water and the meal in the top of a double boiler. Bring the rest of the water to a boil in another pot. When the cornmeal is well blended, add the reserved boiling water and cook until the mixture boils. Add salt. Add enough water in the bottom of the double boiler to barely touch the bottom of the top pan. Bring to a simmer and add the top pan with the mush mixture. Simmer one hour covered. Lastly, add butter or margarine and cheese.

CORNMEAL PANCAKES

Water-ground cornmeal is available either unbolted (whole-grain, with the germ intact) or bolted (almost whole grain). Degerminated cornmeal has the germ (the rudimentary form from which a new organism is developed) removed. Although degerminated cornmeal is less nutritious than unbolted or bolted, it sometimes is enriched to partly compensate for its reduced food value.

Cornmeal provides incomplete protein, calcium, phosphorus, potassium, and magnesium. Incidentally, James J. McDonald, author of *Life in Old Virginia*, wrote, "The colonists got their first taste of Indian corn bread at the Indian village of Kecoughtan -- now Hampton -- on April 30, 1607, 'where [quoting Captain John Smith] they were regaled by the Indians with corn bread, tobacco, and a dance.'"

* * *

1 heaping tsp. baking yeast
1/4 c. warm water
1/4 c. molasses or honey
2 eggs, beaten
1 - 1 1/4 c. milk (or enough to make a thick-as-cream batter)
1 c. cornmeal
1 c. whole wheat flour

Combine in a large bowl the yeast and water. After five minutes, beat in the other liquid ingredients. Add the cornmeal and flour, 1/2 c. at a time, beating out all of the lumps. Stir in the milk. Cover and let rise 20 minutes, or refrigerate overnight, tightly covered.

To cook, lightly oil griddle and ladle on about 1/4 c. batter for each pancake. Bake until bubbles appear and burst on the surface of the pancake, and it is lightly browned. Turn over and cook one minute longer. Yield: 10 large pancakes.

OF BREAD

"The most characteristic hot breads are those which are made from Indian corn. As early as the year 1608, the colonists had gathered Indian corn of their own planting and had learned to make bread of it in the Indian manner, by

mixing cornmeal and water, shaping it into cakes or pones which were baked in hot ashes or on hoes. Of corn pone, the historian, Beverley, wrote in 1705:

'The bread in gentlemen's houses is generally made of wheat, but some rather choose the pone, which is the bread made of Indian meal. Many of the poorer sort of people so little regard the English grain, that though they might have it with the least trouble in the world, yet they don't mind to sow the ground, because they won't be at the trouble of making a fence particularly for it. And, therefore, their constant bread is pone, not so called from the Latin, panis, but from the Indian name Oppone.'

"Although pone (or hoe cakes and ash cakes as they were also called) became the 'constant bread' of the slaves and the poorer people, excellent breads were developed from Indian meal during the seventeenth and eighteenth centuries, which remain in staunch favor today among all classes of Virginians. There are the batter breads (by some, especially those in the more southern colonies, called spoon breads), egg breads, and corn breads . . .

"Of prime importance in the making of these breads is the selection of a proper meal. Only the native corn, ground slowly in a water grist mill may be used and under no circumstances should a cook so far depart from the good judgment of generations of Virginia housewives as to permit sugar in any variety of corn bread."

- by Helen Bullock, author of
The Williamsburg Art of Cookery,
Colonial Williamsburg, 1938, pp. 86-87

BASIC CLASSIC CORN BREAD

Besides cornmeal's use in food, it is also found in laundry starch, sizing for fabrics, paper, and other products.

(It can be sprinkled through the hair and brushed out for a dry shampoo!) It is also found as an ingredient in such industrial products as adhesives, pastes, cleaning products, and soaps. Whole corn, you know, is used in many forms -- ask the folks in the Blue Ridge Mountains of Virginia (and lots of other places, too) about a popular liquid produced from corn!

Better than corn squeezin's is this uncompromisingly good recipe for your basic, classic, quintessentially American corn bread (although it does depart from Helen Bullock's rule against sugar in Virginia corn bread!).

* * *

1 1/2 c. sour milk or buttermilk
2 eggs
1 tbsp. sugar
1/2 tsp. salt
1/2 tsp. baking soda
1 1/2 c. cornmeal
1/2 c. flour
1/4 c. butter or margarine, melted

Beat together the first five ingredients. Stir in cornmeal and flour. Add melted butter. Mix. Pour batter into a greased 8-inch-square pan. Bake at 425° F. for around 25 minutes, or until golden brown.

LOIS ELY'S OLD-FASHIONED CORN BREAD

The Elys operate an old grist mill in Williamsport, Ohio. Here is Lois's yummy corn bread recipe.

* * *

2 c. cornmeal (stone-ground)
1 tsp. soda
1/2 tsp. salt
2 tbsp. sugar (optional)

1 egg
3 tbsp. olive oil (You may use other types of vegetable oil.)
2 c. buttermilk

Sift the first four ingredients. Then beat together the remaining three ingredients. Combine the dry and liquid mixtures. Pour into a hot oiled iron skillet (or muffin tins). Bake at 400° F. for 20 minutes (if in muffin tins) or 25 minutes (if in iron skillet).

SUGAR & SPICE CORN BREAD

In my food research, I came across a recipe for Greek corn bread called "bobota." To me, the use of olive oil, cinnamon, orange juice, and golden raisins in corn bread did indeed sound foreign, but I figured, "Nothing ventured, nothing gained," so we tested it. Amazing! It is excellent! I did modify the recipe somewhat, but the "odd" ingredients are not deleted. (I just changed some proportions and amounts.)

Try this different Sugar & Spice Corn Bread. You'll be "tickled" with it!

* * *

1/4 c. olive oil (or other oil), heated
1 c. yellow cornmeal
1 c. whole wheat, unbleached, or all-purpose flour
1 tbsp. baking powder
1/4 tsp. salt
2 tbsp. sugar
1 tsp. cinnamon
1 c. milk
1 egg, beaten
2 tbsp. thawed orange juice concentrate
1/2 c. golden (or dark) raisins

Combine ingredients in the order given. Stir to moisten thoroughly. Spoon into a greased 8x8-inch Pyrex dish, and bake for 25 minutes at 375° F.

MOLASSES CORN BREAD (OR MUFFINS)

"How do you decide what recipes to put in your cookbooks?" you might ask me. First, I read and study lots of cookbooks belonging to friends, the library, me, etc. I also research foods and recipes of earlier times. Then I narrow in on a particular recipe, and create my own composite list of ingredients from the choices that appeal to me most. After I have this composite recipe, I test it on my brave and willing volunteers, hubby Henry, daughter Sarah, and sons David and Jonathan. My taste-testers are always honest (yet gentle and tactful, in the case of my dud experiments) in telling me what they think of my efforts. If a recipe has potential, but is not perfect, I adjust the ingredients, and re-test, until it suits us. -- So that's how these cookbooks come into being.

Molasses Corn Bread passed the taste-test with flying colors.

* * *

1 1/2 c. bran
1 c. all-purpose flour
1/2 c. cornmeal
1 tbsp. baking powder
1/4 tsp. salt
1/4 c. sugar
1/3 c. vegetable oil
2 eggs, beaten
1 c. milk
1/3 c. molasses

Combine dry ingredients. Add liquids and blend well. Pour into greased 8x8-inch baking dish and bake at 375° F. for 30 minutes; or pour into 18 greased muffin tins and bake at 375° F. for 20 minutes.

APPLE CORN BREAD

The apple adds a surprising taste and texture variation in the following recipe.

3 c. whole wheat flour
1 1/2 c. cornmeal
2 tbsp. baking powder
1 tsp. salt
1/2 c. brown sugar, packed
2 large yellow apples, chopped
2 eggs, beaten
3 c. milk
1/4 c. vegetable oil

Mix dry ingredients. Then mix wet ingredients in a separate container. Combine. Pour into a 8x8 Pyrex dish. Bake at 350° F. for 20-30 minutes, or until firm.

NORTH CAROLINA PONE BISCUITS

North Carolina Pone Biscuits make hearty eating with soup or stew.

* * *

4 c. cornmeal
1 1/2 tsp. salt
2 tbsp. oil
2 1/3 c. boiling water (or more to moisten well)

Combine ingredients. Drop by big spoonfuls onto lightly-greased baking sheets. Bake at 400° F. 15 minutes, turning over if bottoms brown too fast.

COUNTRY SUNSHINE CORNMEAL LOAVES

We love this recipe! I've tried it with white cornmeal, and it tastes fine, but yellow cornmeal makes a more cheerful-looking loaf. [I once read that true Southerners won't touch corn bread made with yellow cornmeal, just as Helen Bullock says true Virginians don't use sweetener in their corn bread. Well, I'm a Southerner, and a Virginian, and I like yellow cornmeal (as well as white) and a little sweetnin', so that shoots those theories!]

* * *

4 c. cornmeal
2 c. flour
2 tsp. baking powder
2 tsp. baking soda
3/4 tsp. salt
1/3 c. sugar
1/3 c. butter or margarine, melted, or vegetable oil
4 c. buttermilk or sour milk

Mix dry ingredients. Stir in butter and buttermilk. Blend well. Pour batter into two greased 9x5-inch loaf pans. Let stand 15 minutes, then bake at 350° F. for 50-60 minutes.

Recently, when I was teaching a group of school-children how to prepare corn pones (in demonstrating Native American and Early American cookery), I asked rhetorically if the students could detect the flavor of corn in our finished product. Many of the youngsters, a lot of whom were city-bred, replied with actual incredulity that "It does taste like corn!" -- Amen!

Because we have tried to wean ourselves from awfully sweet things, the two following brown bread recipes are not as sweet as some . . . . By the way, an old Puritan proverb states, "Brown bread and the Gospel is good and holy fare."

BABETTE'S BOSTON BROWN BREAD

3 c. whole wheat flour
2 1/2 c. cornmeal
1 1/2 tsp. baking soda

2/3 c. molasses
3 - 3 1/4 c. buttermilk or sour milk

Mix together the first three ingredients, then add the molasses and milk. Stir well, and pour into two greased loaf pans. Bake at 350° F. for 40-45 minutes.

BOSTON BROWN BREAD WITH RAISINS

1 c. rye flour
1 c. yellow cornmeal
1 c. whole wheat flour
2 tsp. baking soda
1/4 tsp. salt
3/4 c. raisins
1/3 c. molasses or brown sugar
1 2/3 c. sour milk or buttermilk

Mix the dry ingredients; and in a separate bowl mix the raisins and liquids. Stir together the two mixtures, and fold into a greased 9x5-inch loaf pan. Bake at 350° F. for 45 minutes.

CORNMEAL DROP BISCUITS

Freshly-ground cornmeal keeps nicely in the refrigerator for a week or so. For longer storage, bag in plastic bags (I double-bag) and keep it in the freezer. -- The reason that cornmeal is so perishable is that years of breeding corn for high crop yields has produced a grain that contains lots of polyunsaturated oils. These oils spoil quickly at room temperature.

We are great biscuit fans at the Sims-Mitchell House, especially at breakfast. Um-um-good with honey and/or butter!

* * *

2 c. cornmeal
1/4 c. vegetable oil

3/4 tsp. salt
2 c. milk, hot

1 1/2 c. whole wheat, unbleached, or all-purpose flour
4 tsp. baking powder

Mix together the first four ingredients. Let sit while you combine flour and baking powder. Mix together the two mixtures, and drop by tablespoons on greased baking sheets. Bake at 425° F. about 12 minutes or until lightly browned. Yield will depend on the size of the biscuits you make.

DINNERTIME CORNMEAL ROLLS

Iowa, Illinois, Indiana, Nebraska, Ohio, Missouri, South Dakota, and Minnesota are the leading producers of corn, although it is grown in many other states as well.

In the 1840's, in the United States, there was a grist mill for every 243 people. Much of the grain ground in these grist mills was corn. In our county of Pittsylvania, there were 100 mills (seven of which still stand); and much of their business was devoted to grinding locally-ground corn. -- You can enjoy the "historic" taste of cornmeal in these perfect rolls.

* * *

1/3 c. cornmeal
1/3 c. sugar
1 1/2 tsp. salt
1/2 c. shortening
2 c. milk
1 pkg. baking yeast
1/4 c. warm water
2 eggs, beaten
4 c. flour (or more)
Melted butter
Cornmeal

Combine the 1/3 c. cornmeal with the sugar, salt, shortening, and milk in a saucepan and cook until thickened. Meanwhile, dissolve the yeast in the warm water. When the cornmeal mixture is lukewarm, add the yeast and eggs, and beat well. Stir in enough flour to form a soft dough. Knead on a floured surface. When smooth and springy, place in a bowl; cover; let rise. Punch down and roll out to a 1-inch thickness. Cut with a 2 1/2 - inch biscuit cutter. Brush each unbaked roll with melted butter and dust with cornmeal. Place on a greased baking sheet and cover. Allow to rise until light and fluffy. Bake at 375° F. for 15 minutes. Yield: 18 rolls.

MARY MITCHELL'S SPOON BREAD

My "sentimental favorite" recipe for spoonbread comes from my mother-in-law, Mary Helvey Mitchell. I had the recipe in question and I knew how I prepared it, of course, but I wanted her instructions, since it was an heirloom family dish, so I wrote to her in Bristol, Tennessee. Here's her reply:

"Your note came yesterday -- I hunted up the recipe and found it in my oldest and first cookbook, one I'd written in favorite family recipes. All it said was:

Spoon Bread

1 pint buttermilk
4 eggs
1 tsp. salt
1 tsp. soda
1 c. cornmeal
Small lump of butter

Mix all together and bake in a moderate oven.

"That made a rather large bowl of bread for us, so I had notations on the side for just half the

*recipe, that just fit a small to medium Pyrex bowl
I had. The bowl got broken and I guess I haven't
made spoon bread since.*

*"It might be better to melt the butter and
add it to the mixture -- instead of putting the lump
of butter on top, in the middle, as Grandmother
Thomas, Mother, and I had done."*

*Further note on spoonbread: Some people like to add bits of
ham or bacon, or cracklings, to the batter before baking.
Corn, cheese, herbs, mild or hot peppers, or even blueberries
can also be added for flavor variations.*

ZUCCHINI & COTTAGE CHEESE CORN BREAD

My cooking friend extraordinaire, Helen Edwards
Melton of Hillsville, Virginia, shared with me this Carroll
County special.

* * *

1 1/4 c. self-rising cornmeal
1/4 c. self-rising flour
1 tsp. sugar
1/4 tsp. salt
1 1/4 c. zucchini, peeled and grated
1 medium onion, chopped
3/4 c. cottage cheese
1/4 c. vegetable oil
1 stick margarine, melted
3 eggs, beaten

Mix the dry ingredients. Stir in the remaining things,
and mix well. Pour into a greased 6x10-inch pan, or double
the recipe and use a 9x13-inch pan. Bake at 375° F. for 30
minutes.

ONION CORN BREAD

This indescribably tasty corn bread is a favorite of my husband Henry. It will knock your socks off, and snap your suspenders!

* * *

1 tbsp. each butter and oil
3/4 c. cornmeal
1 egg, beaten
1/3 c. chopped onion
1/2 tsp. baking soda
3/4 tsp. salt
Pinch of pepper
1 c. unflavored yogurt

Put the butter and oil into a 9-inch baking dish and place in a preheated 425° F. oven for the butter to melt. Meanwhile mix all other ingredients in order given. Pour batter into the hot baking dish containing melted fats. Bake at 425° F. for around 25 minutes.

WHOLE WHEAT CORNMEAL SQUARES

Whole Wheat Cornmeal Squares are so satisfying with beans or soup, or as a breakfast bread.

* * *

1 1/3 c. whole wheat flour
1 1/2 c. cornmeal
2 tsp. baking powder
1/4 tsp. salt
2 tbsp. oil
3 tbsp. honey
2 c. milk

Mix the dry things. In a different bowl mix the liquids. Stir together the two mixtures. Pour the batter into a greased 7x11- or 9x13-inch Pyrex dish and bake at 400° F.

for approximately 20 minutes or until the edges start to brown lightly. Cut into squares to serve.

QUICK & EASY BAKED HUSH PUPPIES

Hush puppies are a famous Southern specialty, but are not normally a low-calorie treat; for those who are conscious of the excess fats Americans often consume, this recipe is quite an improvement. The "puppies" are baked in the oven, thus eliminating the copious quantities of grease which fried puppies soak up. Also, this mode of preparation is much less trouble and mess than deep fat frying.

* * *

1 c. cornmeal
1 c. flour, sifted
2 tsp. baking powder
1 tsp. sugar
1/2 tsp. salt
1/8 tsp. cayenne pepper
2 eggs, beaten
3/4 c. milk
1/2 c. onion, minced
1/4 c. vegetable oil

Mix dry ingredients. Add moist ingredients. Spoon into well-greased muffin tins. Bake at 425° F. for 10 to 15 minutes.

CORN DOGS

From hush puppies to corn dogs -- since we were just speaking of good nutrition, I'll have to confess that corn dogs are not a health food. But, for an occasional treat, they are fun. Buy lean wienies, preferably without nitrates, and use whole wheat flour in the coating if desired.

* * *

2/3 c. cornmeal
1/2 c. flour

3/4 tsp. salt
1 egg, beaten
2 tbsp. vegetable oil
1/2 c. milk
One 1-pound pkg. hot dogs

Mix dry ingredients. Mix egg, milk, and oil. Dip each wiener into liquid mixture, then roll in cornmeal mixture. Insert the coated hot dogs onto skewers. Fry dogs a few at a time in hot deep fat (375° F.) until golden brown. Serve with mustard, catsup, or chili sauce.

JALAPENO CORN BREAD

Deep, deep South (would you believe Mexico?)!

* * *

2 c. cornmeal
1 heaping tbsp. flour
1/2 tsp. baking powder
1/2 tsp. soda
3/4 c. buttermilk
1/2 c. vegetable oil
2 eggs, beaten
1 (17-oz.) can cream-style corn
1/2 pound Cheddar cheese, shredded
2 jalapeño peppers, finely chopped
1 onion, chopped
2 cloves garlic, minced
1/2 bell pepper, chopped

Combine dry ingredients. Add other things. Pour into a hot greased 13x9x2-inch baking pan. Bake at 375° F. for about 35 minutes.

PIZZA-MEX

This recipe alone is well worth the price of the cookbook you are holding! I recently developed, tested, and perfected Pizza-Mex; and it was immediately put into our regular rotation of lunch dishes, appearing often on our menu. That means it rates as a top "family favorite!"

A glorious combination of Italian and Mexican foodways, this "bean pizza" with an enchilada taste will please and surprise you and your table-mates, too. (If ya don't like this one, ya better git your taster tested!)

* * *

2 c. cornmeal
1/2 c. flour
3/4 tsp. salt
Boiling water (about 1 1/2 c. or as much as 2 c., depending upon the nature of the grain products, and whether you prefer a crisp or soft crust)
1 c. canned tomato sauce
2 c. cooked pinto beans, drained
1 med. onion, chopped finely
Dash of salt and pepper
2 tbsp. chili powder (or to taste)
Monterey Jack cheese or mozzarella cheese
Plain yogurt (some may prefer sour cream)

Thoroughly mix together the first four ingredients, using enough boiling water to moisten well. Pat this mixture evenly into a 14-inch pizza pan (or make five small pizzas). Score the large pizza into slices. Meanwhile, combine tomato sauce, beans, onion, salt and pepper, and chili powder. Spread sauce over the crust. Bake 15 minutes or until the edges start to turn golden brown. Just before eating, sprinkle on cheese, heat a minute more, then serve. Pass the yogurt to dot on top -- *fire and snow*! Sensationally fabulous!

CORNMEAL PIZZA CRUST

Here is a way to add a distinctively American twist to the traditional Italian pizza.

* * *

1 tbsp. baking yeast
1 c. warm water
2 tbsp. oil
1/4 tsp. salt
1/2 c. cornmeal
Approximately 3 c. whole wheat flour

Dissolve yeast in the water. When it bubbles, add remaining ingredients. Stir well, then knead until smooth and elastic (about five minutes). Put into a greased bowl, turning to grease all sides. Cover and let rise about 1 1/2 hours. Punch down. Divide in half and place each half on a greased 12- to 14-inch pizza pan. Push dough to the edges of the pans, forming a rim around the outside. At this point, add your choice of sauce and toppings, and bake at 425° F. for 15 to 20 minutes. Yield: 2 pizzas.

QUICKY CORNMEAL PIZZA CRUST

When my husband and I were at Virginia Tech, and not yet married, pizza was a high point of our existence. What joy to skip one of the notoriously dismal meals at the college, and go eat pizza at the infamously romantic Duck Pond! We usually ordered two medium pizzas -- one sausage and one cheese -- often from the Hokie House, or the now-long-gone pizza shack over near the Wesley Foundation; two large soft drinks; and, if we were *really* celebrating something, we'd drive out to Radford Brothers Grocery and purchase a couple of apples or pears. After gathering our feast, we would head over to the Duck Pond (not too bawdy a place in broad daylight) and happily stuff our faces.

I still love to eat pizza with my sweetie! -- And with this recipe, you don't even have to wait for the yeast to do its work.

* * *

1/2 c. cornmeal
1 3/4 c. all-purpose, unbleached, or whole wheat flour
1 tsp. baking powder
1/4 tsp. salt

3/4 c. milk
2 tbsp. vegetable oil

Combine dry ingredients. Mix in milk and oil. Using your hands, work into a ball (it may be necessary to add additional flour to achieve the proper dough consistency). Roll out on a floured surface. Place in a 14-inch pizza pan. Trim off extra dough with kitchen scissors. Add sauce and toppings and bake at 425° F. for 15-20 minutes.

CHEESY CORNMEAL CRACKERS

It took me awhile to realize that I could make delicious crackers at home. I had to find satisfactory recipes, and then alot the time necessary to carry out the project. Homemade crackers are worth the effort! They contain no strange-sounding chemicals or preservatives as do most store-bought brands. Baked-at-home crackers are health-builders when they contain wholesome whole grain products. We often eat a tossed salad as a first course at dinner, and crackers are a perfect "go-along-with."

* * *

1 c. cornmeal
1/2 c. whole wheat flour
1/4 tsp. salt
1/4 tsp. baking soda
1/4 tsp. chili powder
2 tbsp. grated Cheddar cheese
2 tbsp. vegetable oil
1/2 c. buttermilk or sour milk

Combine the dry ingredients. Stir in cheese, vegetable oil, and buttermilk or sour milk. Work into a ball, and on a floured surface roll out very thinly. Cut out crackers (they do not all have to be perfectly square!). Prick each cracker with a fork a couple of times. Bake at 350° F. for 8 to 10 minutes on a greased baking sheet. Watch carefully; it's easy to burn them.

THE MAN WHO HAS CORN

"The man who has it [corn] has everything; he can sow the land with it, and for the rest everything eats corn, from slave to chick."

- *by Harriet Martineau, quoted by Otto Bettmann in* **The Good Old Days - They Were Terrible!**

SESAME-CORNMEAL CRACKERS

Zea mays (corn) is the chief grain crop of the United States (much of the yield is used as animal feed). In world grain production, corn ranks behind rice and wheat. There are numerous varieties of corn grown today. Some cornstalks reach heights of 20 feet or more, and some mature ears of corn are two feet long! Hybrid corn is often ground for cornmeal. Cornmeal is available in varying textures, from coarsely ground to finely ground. -- It seems to me that coarsely ground meal has a more pronounced corn flavor; and, for some reason, coarse cornmeal produces a lighter product than finely ground cornmeal. Try it and see!

These Sesame-Cornmeal Crackers are best heated in the oven just prior to serving. They are crisp and have a definite corn flavor, almost like corn chips.

* * *

3 c. whole wheat flour
1 c. cornmeal
1/2 tsp. salt
1/2 c. vegetable oil
Water
Sesame seeds

Combine flour, cornmeal, salt, oil, and enough water to make a workable dough. Knead lightly and roll out very thinly on a floured surface. Sprinkle sesame seeds over the dough, and with a rolling pin press them into the dough. Cut into squares or rectangles or whatever shape you like and bake at 375° F. for around 15 minutes, watching closely so as not to burn them.

A-MAIZE-ING-LY GOOD TUNA PATTIES

A speedy-to-fix, enjoyable-to-eat lunch or supper entree, these tuna patties are enhanced by the addition of cornmeal.

* * *

1/2 c. Creamy Chicken Mushroom Soup
2 cans (7 oz. each) tuna, drained
1/2 c. cornmeal
1 egg, slightly beaten
1/2 c. onion, minced

Combine the above ingredients and form six patties. In a skillet, brown patties in melted butter or margarine. Serve with tomato sauce, catsup, or make a sauce by heating together the remainder of the canned soup and 3/4 c. milk.

Note: The term "maize" apparently comes from a West Indian word, "mahiz," meaning "our life." Corn is important to our lives. Besides cornmeal we enjoy grits and hominy. Finely-milled corn flour is used in commercial breakfast foods; and in Louisiana it is used to bread seafood and vegetables for frying. Now researchers have developed no-calorie, high-fiber corncob flour!

The two following dressings are excellent accompaniments to turkey or chicken. Roast turkey is appealing year-round, so don't just serve it at Thanksgiving and/or Christmas.

SIMPLE PLEASURES CORN BREAD DRESSING

3 1/2 c. corn bread crumbs
3 1/2 c. bread or biscuit crumbs
1/4 c. butter or margarine
1 med. onion, chopped
1 c. celery, chopped
1 egg, beaten
1/3 c. milk
1 1/2 tsp. salt
1/2 tsp. pepper
1 tbsp. sage
4 hard-cooked eggs, chopped (optional)
2 c. chicken or turkey broth, or water

Mix crumbs in a large bowl. Sauté onions and celery in butter. Add all ingredients to the crumbs, and mix well. Spoon into a shallow greased pan and bake at 400° F. for about 30 minutes.

HIT-THE-JACKPOT CORN BREAD 'N' OYSTER DRESSING

6 c. corn bread crumbs
3/4 c. butter or margarine
1 c. onion, chopped
1 c. celery, chopped
Up to 1 quart oysters, drained (reserve liquid)
Salt and pepper
Turkey stock

Sauté onion and celery in butter. Add oysters, and heat until the edges curl. Combine with corn bread, salt, and pepper. Moisten with oyster liquid and turkey stock. Spoon into a greased baking pan and bake at 400° F. for 30 minutes.

HACIENDA TAMALE PIE

Tamale pie seems to have been one of the first Mexican foods to become popular in the United States (at least east of the Mississippi). Let's turn back the pages of time and feast on that Mexican import -- a bean or meat/corn/tomato mixture topped with a cornmeal crust.

* * *

1/2 lb. ground beef, cooked and drained, or
      2 c. cooked beans (kidney or other)
1 c. canned tomato sauce
1/2 c. green pepper, chopped
1 med. onion, chopped
1/4 tsp. salt
1/4 tsp. oregano
2 tsp. chili powder
Dash of garlic powder
1 c. whole kernel corn
1 c. sharp Cheddar cheese, grated (optional)
1/4 c. black olives, diced (optional)

Combine the above ingredients in a saucepan and simmer for about 15 minutes. Meanwhile, make **Cornmeal Topping:**

3/4 c. cornmeal
2 tbsp. flour
1/4 tsp. salt
1/2 c. milk
1 tbsp. vegetable oil

Mix cornmeal, flour, and salt. Stir in milk and vegetable oil. Beat out lumps.

Spoon the meat/tomato mixture into a 9x9x2-inch baking dish. Spoon on cornmeal topping. Bake at 375° F. for 30 minutes. Yield: 4-6 servings.

INDIAN PUDDING

Like the early settlers who originally enjoyed Indian Pudding, our goal is that our home be a happy and safe refuge from the outside world. The heart of our big old house, and a magnet for the whole family, is the large, rustic kitchen. Often there is something cooking, emanating warmth and aroma; we do home schooling in that room; Henry works at the kitchen table there; the children play there. As you partake of Indian Pudding, remember and resolve to recapture the strength and stability of the family unit when this nation began!

* * *

4 c. milk
2/3 c. cornmeal
1/4 tsp. salt
1 egg, beaten
1/4 c. butter or margarine
1/3 c. molasses
1/4 c. sugar
1/2 tsp. each cinnamon and ginger (optional)
A dash of nutmeg (optional)

Scald 3 cups of milk in a large pot. Meanwhile, mix cornmeal, salt, and the remaining cup of milk. Stir into the scalded milk, bringing it to a boil, and stirring all the while. Reduce heat to low, and cook five minutes, stirring occasionally. Remove from heat.

Stir in egg, butter, molasses, sugar, and spices (if desired). Pour into a greased 1 1/2 - quart casserole dish. Set the dish in a baking pan and pour boiling water into the pan to within one inch of the top of the casserole dish. Bake uncovered at 275° F. for three hours.

Serve still warm with milk or ice cream.